BY

JOHN NICHOLSON,

AUTHOR OF "FOLK MOOTS"

(Hon. Treasurer Hull Literary Club).

ONE SHILLING AND SIXPENCE.

HULL: A. BROWN AND SONS, SAVILE STREET.
LONDON: SIMPKIN, MARSHALL, AND CO.
DRIFFIELD: T. HOLDERNESS, "OBSERVER" OFFICE.
1887.

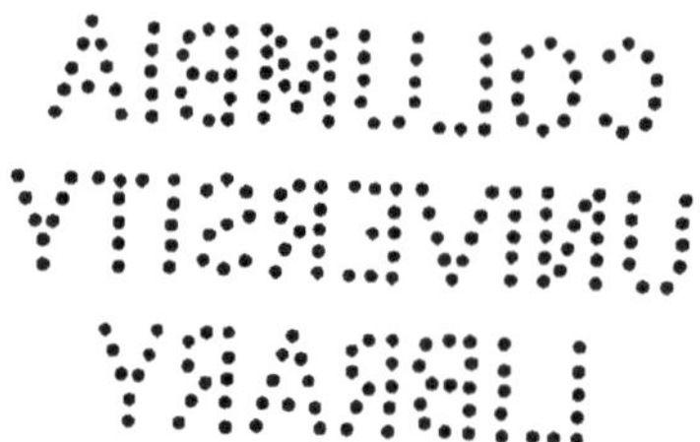

(One Hundred Large Paper Copies have been printed, at Five Shillings each, and can be obtained only of the Author, 33, Leicester Street, Hull.)

THOS. HOLDERNESS, PRINTER, DRIFFIELD.

TO

WILLIAM HUNT, Esq.,

PRESIDENT OF THE HULL LITERARY CLUB,

THIS TRIBUTE OF ESTEEM

IS RESPECTFULLY DEDICATED

BY THE AUTHOR.

PREFACE.

THE greater part of this booklet was read before the members of the Hull Literary Club, on the 1st of November, 1886, under the presidency of Wm. Hunt, Esq.

The author begs to acknowledge his indebtedness to the following gentlemen for their assistance in gathering and supplying information, which otherwise would have been unattainable; and for kindnesses which have been generous and unceasing.

Rev. J. W. Stanbridge, M.A., Rector of Bainton.
Lewis L. Kropf, Esq., Hull.
Rev. H. E. Maddock, M.A., Vicar of Patrington.
Rev. Canon Taylor, M.A., LL.D. Rector of Settrington.
Rev. G. N. Herbert, M.A., Rector of Cowlam.
Rev. G. G. Holmes, B.D., Vicar of Holme.
Rev. R. D. C. Cordeaux, B.A., Vicar of Paull.
Rev. T. W. Kelly, B.A., Vicar of Mapleton.
Rev. Ed. Mitford, M.A., Vicar of Muston.
Rev. J. A. Eldridge, M.A., Vicar of Bishop Wilton.

Rev. C. S. Booty, M.A., Vicar of Rudston.
H. W. Bainton, Esq., Arram Hall.
Wm. Andrews, Esq., F. R. H. S., Hon. Sec. Hull Literary Club.
Simpson Staveley, Esq., Eastlands, Tibthorpe.
Richard Wood, M.D., Driffield.
E. S. Wilson, Esq., F.S.A., Trinity House, Hull.
Jno. Browne, Esq., Bridlington Quay.
Hy. Angas, Esq., Driffield.
J. R. Mortimer, Esq., Driffield.
Thos. Boynton, Esq., Ulrome Grange, Ulrome.
Bielby Topham, Esq., Manor House, Bainton.
Edwd. Newdegate, Esq., Barmston.
W. G. B. Page, Esq., Royal Institution, Hull.
Thos. Todd, Esq., Wressle Castle.
H. A. Lee, Esq., Speeton.

33, Leicester Street, Hull,
November, 1886.

CONTENTS.

ILLUSTRATIONS.

LIST OF WORKS CONSULTED.

Geology of Yorkshire, by John Phillips, F.G.S. (York: Thos. Wilson and Son).

A Short History of the English People, by John Richard Green. (London: Macmillan).

The Fifteen Decisive Battles of the World, by Sir Ed. Creasy, M.A. (London: Bentley and Son).

The History and Antiquities of Holderness, by Geo. Poulson. (Hull: Robert Brown).

Modern Yorkshire Poets, by William Andrews, F.R.H.S. (London: Simpkin, Marshall, and Co.)

History of Wressle, by J. Savage. (London: H. D. Symonds).

Book of Days. (London: Chambers).

Lays of Ancient Rome, by Lord Macaulay. (London: Longmans).

Map of East Yorkshire (temp. Elizabeth), by kind permission of E. S. Wilson, Esq., F.S.A., Hull.

Map of East Riding of Yorkshire from Actual Survey, by A. Bryant, in the years 1827 and 1828. (London: A. Bryant, 1829). By kind permission of James Oldham, Esq., C.E., Hull.

Map of Yorkshire, constructed from Actual Survey and corrected in the years 1834-5. (London: H. Teesdale and Co., 21st October, 1835). A copy of this map hangs in the Reading Room of the Young People's Institute, Charlotte Street, Hull.

Sundry Sheets of the 6 inch Yorkshire Ordnance Survey.

Britannia Depicta, 1736. By kind permission of John Brown, Esq., Hull.

BEACONS OF EAST YORKSHIRE.

CHAPTER I.

THE SPANISH ARMADA.

BEACON, from Anglo Saxon beácen or beácn, a sign or token, and is thus akin to "beckon," to make a signal.

Lord Coke says that "the erection of beacons, lighthouses, and sea marks is a branch of the Royal Prerogative; the first whereof was anciently used to alarm the country in case of the approach of an enemy; and all of them are signally useful in guiding and preserving vessels at sea, by night as well as day. For this purpose the king hath the exclusive power, by Commission under his great seal, to cause them to be erected in fit and convenient places, as well upon the lands of the subject, as upon the demesnes of the Crown, which power is usually vested by letters patent in the office of the High Admiral or the Admiralty Board." Further, in his Fourth Institute, chap. xxv., it is said, "Before the reign of Edward III., the beacons were but stacks of wood set up on high places, which were fired when the coming of enemies was descried; but in his reign, pitch-boxes, as now they be, were, instead of these stacks, set up; and this properly is a beacon."

In Poulson's "Holderness,"* there is a map of Hornsea Mere, on which a beacon is marked, a few hundred yards to the north of the Stream Dike. It consists of an arrangement like a gallows-tree, from which is suspended an object, that looks like a pitch-pot; but the sketch is too small, and too much in want of detail, to draw a correct conclusion.

Fires by night, as signals to convey, with the greatest expedition, the notice of danger to distant places, have been used in many countries and in all ages: but in the present work the writer intends to deal only with those of our own land, and chiefly with those of the East Riding of Yorkshire.

The original edition of "The Lay of the Last Minstrel" contains a note to the effect that "The border beacons, from their number and position, formed a sort of telegraphic communication with Edinburgh. The Act of Parliament, 1455, c. 48, directs that one bale or faggot shall be a warning of the approach of the English in any manner; two bales, that they are *coming indeed*; four bales, blazing beside each other, that the enemy are in great force. 'The same taikenings to be watched and maid at Eggerhope Castle, fra they se the fire of Hume, that they fire richt swa. And in like manner on Sowtra Edge, [they] sall se the fire of Eggerhope Castell, and mak taikening in like maner: And then may all Louthiane be warned, and in special the Castel of Edinburgh; and their four fires to be maid in like maner; that they in Fife, and fra Striviling east, and the east part of Louthiane, and to Dunbar, all may se them and come to the defense of the realme.' These beacons (at least in later times) were a 'long and strong tree set up, with a long iron pole across the head of it, and an iron brander † fixed on a stalk in the middle of it, for holding a tar-barrel.'"

The tax to support these, and permanent navigation

* Vol I., p. 435.

† Cage, cresset, tripod. See Rudston Beacon.

beacons, was called "Beaconage," and was levied by the sheriff, on the hundred in which they were situated.

In the history of our country there have been two occasions when the fear of foreign invasion lay on the country like a nightmare. But, though the fear was great, and the danger serious and imminent, British courage rose with the danger. The peril united brave hearts and willing hands, and these times of national unity and enthusiasm will bear comparison with the most heroic times of any country in any age. The plan and result of these two threatened invasions were very similar. What the Spaniard attempted in the 16th century, the Frenchman tried to do in the 19th; the failure of Philip was repeated by Napoleon three hundred years after. Each provided an immense army of invasion, thousands of transport vessels, and a powerful fleet for defence and convoy of the same.

"As Napoleon, in 1805, waited with his army and flotilla at Boulogne, looking for Villeneuve to drive away the English cruisers, and secure him a passage across the Channel, so Parma, in 1588, waited for Medina Sidonia to drive away the Dutch and English squadrons that watched his flotilla, to enable his veterans to cross the sea to the land that they were to conquer. Thanks to Providence, in each case England's enemy waited in vain!" *

On the 1st day of September, 1586, Sir George Carew, Governor of the Isle of Wight, issued "Instructions for every centioner to observe duringe the continuance of the Spanish Fleet uppon this cost, untill knowledge shal be had of ther dispercement.

"Imprimis, that all the beacons, especially thos of the est and west forlands be dubled, and garded with such watchmen as shal be of judgement and discretion; uppon the fyrst occasion of approche offered by the ennymie to rayse

* Creasy's "Decisive Battles," p 239.

the laram by bells or hoblers;* and yf they shall procead forthe to landing to fyer the beacons.

"That yow appoynt the serchers of every beacon diligentlye to attend ther charge from tyme to tyme, to advertis yow what the centioners shal descry, and that uppon any matter discovered yow advertis me with diligens what shal be seen.

"That yow appoynt the beacons sufficientlie to be supplied with fuell, and that yow appoynt for every day-watch a gare,† reddy, uppon the first occasion to be hanged up.

"That yow order in all the perrishes within your canten, that no bells be ronge in the church for service, christeninge, or burriall, but only one bell during this time, and uppon the alaram al the bells to be ronge out.

"That yow appoynt som of your hoblers during this tyme stil to attend yow, and that their horses be alwais in reddiness to pass in hast as occasion shal be offred.

"That yow charge al your centioners (as they wil answer to the contraire at their perills) to provide themselves with powder, shott, and matche sufficient; and that they be in a reddiness uppon the first strocke of an alaram, to marche to the place of their fyrst assemblie, but that al that can, com on horsebacke, repayring in al haste to meet me at the place from whence the alaram shal be fyrst raysed.

"That every man carry into the fielde with him, when he goethe abroad, his furniture that he may the soner be in a reddiness to answer the alaram.

"That every househoulder make provision in a reddiness of meale or bread for one monthe, according to the proportion of his houshoulde, that we may keep the fielde yf wee shall se occasion.

"That yow observe, as well in watching and firinge of beacons, as in other occasionns of servic presented at this

* Horsemen. † Notice to beware.

time in my former booke of instructions, and consider well the contens thereof.

"*(Signed)* George Carey.

"This to pass from Mr. Dingley to Mr. Erlsman, Mr. John Basket to Mr. Bourinniam from hande to hande in post." *

In Macaulay's Ballad on the Spanish Armada, the transmission of the tidings of the Armada's approach, and the arming of the English nation, are magnificently described:

THE ARMADA. †

[A FRAGMENT.]

Attend, all ye who list to hear our noble England's praise;
I tell of the thrice famous deeds she wrought in ancient days,
When that great fleet invincible against her bore in vain
The richest spoils of Mexico, the stoutest hearts of Spain.

It was about the lovely close of a warm summer day,
There came a gallant merchant-ship full sail to Plymouth Bay;
Her crew had seen Castile's black fleet, beyond Aurigny's Isle,
At earliest twilight, on the waves lie heaving many a mile.
At sunrise she escaped their van, by God's especial grace;
And the tall *Pinta*, till the noon, had held her close in chase.
Forthwith a guard at every gun was placed along the wall;
The beacon blazed upon the roof of Edgecumbe's lofty hall;
Many a light fishing bark put out to pry along the coast,
And with loose rein and bloody spur rode inland many a post.

* Archæologia, Vol. 13, p. 100.
† By permission of Messrs. Longmans.

With his white hair unbonneted, the stout old sheriff comes;
Behind him march the halberdiers, before him sound the drums;
His yeomen round the market cross make clear an ample space,
For there behoves him to set up the standard of Her Grace.
And haughtily the trumpets peal, and gaily dance the bells,
As slow upon the labouring wind the royal blazon swells.
Look how the Lion of the sea lifts up his ancient crown,
And underneath his deadly paw treads the gay lilies down.
So stalked he when he turned to flight, on that famed Picard field,
Bohemia's plume, and Genoa's bow, and Cæsar's eagle shield.
So glared he when at Agincourt in wrath he turned to bay,
And crushed and torn beneath his claws, the princely hunters lay.
Ho! strike the flagstaff deep, Sir Knight; ho! scatter flowers, fair maids;
Ho! gunners, fire a loud salute; ho! gallants, draw your blades;
Thou sun, shine on her joyously; ye breezes, waft her wide:
Our glorious SEMPER EADEM, the banner of our pride.
The freshening breeze of eve unfurled that banner's massy fold;
The parting gleam of sunshine kissed that haughty scroll of gold;
Night sank upon the dusky beach, and on the purple sea,
Such night in England ne'er had been, nor e'er again shall be.
From Eddystone to Berwick bounds, from Lynn to Milford Bay,
That time of slumber was as bright and busy as the day;
For swift to east and swift to west the ghastly warflame spread,
High on St. Michael's Mount it shone: it shone on Beachy Head.
Far on the deep the Spaniard saw, along each southern shire,
Cape beyond cape, in endless range, those twinkling points of fire.
The fisher left his skiff to rock on Tamar's glittering waves;
The rugged miners poured to war from Mendip's sunless caves;
O'er Longleat's towers, o'er Cranbourne's oaks, the fiery herald flew,
He roused the shepherds of Stonehenge, the rangers of Beaulieu.

Right sharp and quick the bells all night rang out from Bristol
town,
And ere the day three hundred horse had met on Clifton down.
The sentinel on Whitehall gate looked forth into the night,
And saw o'erhanging Richmond Hill the streak of blood-red light.
Then bugle's note and cannon's roar the death-like silence broke,
And with one start, and with one cry, the royal city woke.
At once on all her stately gates arose the answering fires;
At once the wild alarum clashed from all her reeling spires;
From all the batteries of the Tower pealed loud the voice of fear;
And all the thousand masts of Thames sent back a louder cheer;
And from the furthest wards was heard the rush of hurrying feet,
And the broad streams of pikes and flags rushed down each roar-
ing street;
And broader still became the blaze, and louder still the din,
As fast from every village round the horse came spurring in;
And eastward straight from wild Blackheath the war-like errand
went,
And roused in many an ancient hall the gallant squires of Kent.
Southward from Surrey's pleasant hills flew those bright couriers
forth;
High on bleak Hampstead's swarthy moor they started for the
north,
And on, and on, without a pause, untired they bounded still,
All night from tower to tower they sprang; they sprang from hill
to hill,
Till the proud Peak unfurled the flag o'er Darwin's rocky dales;
Till like volcanoes flared to heaven the stormy hills of Wales;
Till twelve fair counties saw the blaze on Malvern's lonely height;
Till streamed in crimson on the wind the Wrekin's crest of light;
Till broad and fierce the star came forth on Ely's stately fane,
And tower and hamlet rose in arms o'er all the boundless plain;
Till Belvoir's lordly terraces the sign to Lincoln sent,
And Lincoln sped the message on o'er the wide vale of Trent;

Till Skiddaw saw the fire that burned on Gaunt's embattled pile,
And the red glare on Skiddaw roused the burghers of Carlisle.

Had the colossal armament made its first appearance off Spurn instead of the Lizard, its approach would have been as quickly announced, for the following certificate of the number of beacons in East Yorkshire, made in 1588, in response to the inquiry of Elizabeth as to the state of the beacons, shews that the district was well supplied with the means of signalling the danger.

"The justices of the East Riding certified that there were in

DICKERING, XIX. BEACONS.

BRIDLINGTON-CUM-KEY three beacons uppon the sea cost, geving lighte to Flambroughe and Fraistroppe.

FLAMBROUGH, three beacons uppon the sea cost, takinge lighte from Bridlington, and geving lighte to Rudstone.

MUSTON, three beacons half a myll from the sea cost, taking lighte from Righton, and geveth lighte to Staxton.

RIGHTON-CUM-SPETONN, three beacons on the sea cost, takinge lighte from Flambroughe, and geveth light to Rudstone.

RUDSTONE, two beacons foure mylls from the sea cost, taketh lighte from Flambroughe and Righton, and geveth light to Ruston.

RUSTON BEACON, six mylls from the sea cost, taketh lighte from Rudstone, and giveth lighte to Bainton beacon.

FRAISTROPPE-CUM-AWBURNE, 3 beacons a myll from the sea, taketh lighte from Bridlington, and geveth lighte to Houlderness.

STAXTON BEACON, taketh light from Muston, and geveth light to Coleham.

BUCKROSE, II. BEACONS.

COLEHAM, (Cowlam) one beacon, takinge lighte from

Staxton and Bridlington, and geveth lighte to Settrington. Some affirm that yt may be sene as farre as Hornsey in Houlderness.

Settrington beacon, taketh lighte at Coleham and Scarbrough, and geveth lighte to Whitwell beacon, and all that way to Yorke, and into Harthill, and over the most part of Pickering Lythe.

HARTHILL, VI. BEACONS.

Hunsley, two beacons takinge lighte from Bainton, and geveth lighte to Holme.

Bainton, two beacons takinge lighte from Ruston, and geveth lighte to Hunsley and Wilton.

Wilton beacon taketh lighte from Bainton, Hunsley, and Ruston, and giveth lighte to Holme beacon, to the cytty of York, and to the lowe Cuntreye.

Holme beacon taketh lighte from Hunsley and Wilton, and geveth lighte to Marchland and the Lowe Cuntreyes.

HOULDERNESS.

Kilneseye, three beacons Dimilton ,, Withornese ,, Waxholme ,, Grimeston ,,	All uppon the sea cost, and do geve light to these beacons following uppon Humber.
Welwicke Patrington Bovverhouse-hill Paulle Marfleet	The beacons standinge uppon Humber and takinge lighte from the beacons aforesaid, do geve lighte to the beacons in Hartil and Hulshier, which are Transbye (Tranby) and Hunslay.

Further upon the sea cost in Houlderness.

Awbrough	three beacons	Those give lighte to Bainton and Rudstone.
Mappleton	"	
Hornsey	"	
Skipsay	"	
Barnstone	"	

OWSE AND DARWINE.

In Owse and Darwine, it is certified that there are not anie beacons.

"Orders to be observed for the watching of the Beacons in Houlderness and other parts of the East Rydinge.

"TO FYRE ONE BEACON.

"First, that the beacons be watched dilligentlie, and that there be a certain number of the wisest and discretest men dwellinge within the limitts of everie beacon-place, one of them at the least every daie and every night, being assotiate with a reasonable number of other personns; that is to say, that there be every daie two persons, and everie night three persons, and none be allowed to watch but honest householders, and above the age of 30 yeres, except he be specialli elected and appointed by name.

"Item: that yff the said watchmen se or discerne anie shipps on the sea, or in the ryver of Humber, which by there stay, or alteration of there course or otherwise, do geve plain occasion of suspicion to be enemies, and doubtful to do some harme eyther on the maine lande, or to some of oure shippes saylinge alongst the coste on the sea; that then the said watchmen, with the advice and direction of some of the wisest and discretest men appointed as is aforesaid, shall sett on fire one of the beacons onlie, to the intente not onlie to geve oure shippes on the sea warning of the enimie, but also to be a warninge to the people of the cuntrey, that they look the better about them, and be the more redie as occasion shall serve, and that none of the beacons within the lande (when there is but two together) shall be sett on fyre, for the fyreinge of one beacon onlie uppon the shore.

"TO FYRE TWO BEACONS.

"Item: yf the said watchmen do se or discerne anie great number of shippes, which by the course aforesaid, or otherwise, do geve vehement suspicion to be enemies, and to be doubted that they mean to invade; that then they shall with the advice aforesaid, sett two of the said thre beacons (standing together) on fyre, where uppon the watchmen within the mayne land, where two beacons be together, shall onlie sett fyre one of the said two beacons to the intent, that every man in charge put himself in armoure and be redy.

"TO FYRE THREE BEACONS.

"Item: yf the said watchmen on the sea coste (or Humber) do see any greate number of shippes which to them is apparant to be enimies, and that they offer and do come of land to invade, that then the said watchmen (where three beacons be together) shall sett all there three beacons on fier, upon sight whereof, the watchmen within the lande (where two beacons be together) shall fyer both there beacons. And, that farther within the land (where there is but one beacon in the place) the watchmen shall sett the same on fyer, to the intente to geve warninge and knowledge of the present danger, and that there uppon, every man in charge may resorte with all speed to the place or shore from whence the fyrst lighte was given, as shall be thought meet by the General or cheife leader.

"Item: if there be anie occasion of fieringe of beacons within the east end of Houlderness, or alongst the sea cost that then every one of them take there lighte at others, as followeth: from Kilnsey to Welwike beacons; from Wellwike to Patrington beacons; from Patrington to the beacon field, or the Bowerhouse-hill beacons; from thence to Pawll beacons; from Pawll to Marfleet beacons; from Marfleet (which is the westermost beacon in Houlderness) the two beacons of Tranbie shall take there light, and from thence along the ryver of Humber. And lykewise the two beacons at Hunsley, shall take there light from Pawll, and other the beacons on the shore of Humber, and geve lighte to the Holme beacone; and from Holme beacone west warde.

"Item: yf anie occasion, as is aforesaid, of fyeringe of beacons be on the Northe parte of Houlderness, or within the weapontake of Dickering, where three beacons stand together, that then they shall take there lighte one at another; viz.—from anie of the beacons on the sea cost or shore to Staxton beacons, from Staxton to Settrington beacon, from thence to Whitwell beacon, and also from Hornsey and Barmeston, or any of the beacons on that parte.

"Rudstone beacon shall take his lighte from Ruston to Coleham, from Coleham to Wilton, and so into the Lowe Cuntrey; and likewise from Hornsey or other the beacons on the shore. Baynton Beacon doth take his lighte from Baynton to Wilton, and so towards Yorke and the upper parte of the cuntrey.

"Item: that there be provided for every beacon half a tar barrell, at the least; and for everie three beacons standing together there, three half barrells to spare, to the end that yf by occasion, anie of the barrells be spent by reason of fyreinge of one beacon onlie, or two (upon that small occasion) that then the reast may be redy for that purpose, when they shall be forced to sett more than one on fyer; and that the same barells be left in the kepeinge of some honest, substantiall man, dwellinge niest or neare unto the said beacons.

"Item: that the people of the cuntrey having warninge that the same invasion be on the sea coste, that then all the catell, shepe, horse, and victual, be carried, and driven from thence where the enimie shall be, into the mayn land; and that everie man do his best endevore to the uttermoste of his power to prevent the enemie of all victualls, or other commodities which by anie means maie stand them in steade."

East Yorkshire also provided 21 light horsemen, and 1,600 footmen to resist the landing or progress of the Spaniard. *

RUDSTONE in 1588 had "two beacons, foure mylls from the sea cost, which taketh lighte from Flambroughe and Righton and geveth light to Ruston." Respecting these beacons, the Vicar of Rudston (Rev. C. S. Booty) kindly supplied me with the following "Extract from Rudstone Parish Registers respecting beacons.

"A note of such towns as are charged with ye repairing of the Beacons at many howes in Rudstone field, as followeth:—

"Rudston, Thorp, and Carethorp are to find the Standers.

"Langtoft and Cottham, or Cotton, the stakes.

"Burton Agnes, the pinns and whinns.

"Killham, ye Barrels and Brandriths. †

"Thornham and Haisthorp, ye fire, and to keep it burning.

"*(Signed)* THOMAS PIERSON,
"Vicar of Rudston,
"1573."

E. S. Wilson, Esq., F.S.A., Hull, has in his possession a map of Holderness (*temp.* Queen Eliz.) which he kindly allowed me to examine. On it are marked all the beacons above mentioned, with their cressets filled with flaming material. They are much the shape of Dimlington Beacon

* Poulson's "Holderness," Vol. I., p. 85.

† The brandrith is literally an iron tripod, and would be the grate to hold the barrel of tar, under which was placed a small whin busk or gorse bush, a fierce burning and highly inflammable material. It was meet that Burton Agnes should find the whins, for until about 80 years ago, the greater part of the parish was covered with whins, which were pared off the land, and burnt, before the land could be cultivated.

save that the bottom of the cage is flat, instead of concave. Since these sketches were made, fault has been found with the roundness of the cage bottom, as being neither so safe nor suitable as the flat bottoms; but the objection has not been advanced by those who have sketched, verified, or who had seen the beacons when in existence.

Drake's "singeing of the Spanish King's beard," the death of Santa Cruz, the Spanish Admiral, and the winter storms, delayed the sailing of the Armada till the spring of 1588, and it had hardly started when a gale in the Bay of Biscay drove its shattered vessels into Ferrol. It was only on the 29th of July that the sails of the Armada were seen from the Lizard, and the English beacons flared out their alarm along the coast. The news found England ready. To secure a landing at all, the Spaniards had to be masters of the Channel; and in the Channel lay an English fleet resolved to struggle hard for the mastery. The forces were strangely unequal, in numbers, in size of ships, in armaments and crews. But the English ships were in perfect trim. They sailed two feet for the Spaniards one, and closing in and drawing off as they would, hung boldly on the rear of the great fleet as it moved along the Channel. "The feathers of the Spaniard are being plucked, one by one," said the English seamen, as galleon after galleon was sunk, boarded, or driven on shore. Now halting, now moving slowly on, the running fight lasted throughout the week, till the Armada dropped anchor in Calais Roads, with its largest ships ranged outside like "strong castles fearing no assault; the lesser vessels placed in the middle ward." The time had now come for sharper work if the junction of the Armada with Parma was to be prevented; for, demoralized as the Spaniards had been by the merciless chase, their loss in ships had not been great, while the English supplies of food and ammunition were fast running out. Howard resolved to force an engagement; and, lighting eight fire ships at midnight sent them down with the tide upon the Spanish line. The galleons at once cut their cables, and stood out in panic to sea, driving with the wind in a long line off Gravelines. Now was the golden opportunity, and nobly was that opportunity used. Drake was one of the first to close in, and at dawn nearly all the English ships had closely followed, spending almost their last cartridge ere the sun went down. Some of the galleons had sunk, some had drifted helplessly ashore, but the bulk remained, and Drake said the fleet seemed "wonderful great and strong;" but within the Armada all hope was gone. Huddled together by the wind and the deadly English fire, their sails torn, their masts shot away, the crowded galleons had become mere slaughter houses; and as they were driven away past Dunkirk, Drake said, "Parma must have chafed like a bear robbed of her whelps." The Spanish Admiral, despairing of success, fled northward with a southerly wind in the hope of rounding Scotland and Ireland and so returning to Spain without a further encounter with the English fleet. The storms of the northern seas completed their destruction, for only one third ever reached home again, which they had quitted in such pageantry and pride. In the words of Drake "they did not in all their sailing round about England so much as sink or take one ship, bark, pinnace, or cock boat of ours, or even burn so much as one sheep cote on this land." *

* Green's "Short History" (p. 409) and Creasy's "Decisive Battles" (p. 245).

CHAPTER II.

A THREATENED INVASION.

FOR some two hundred years after the defeat of the Spanish Armada, the land had peace from foreign invasion, when again, towards the end of the last century, our great grand parents were terribly alarmed by Napoleon's threatened invasion. Only those who have lived during the anxious years, or who have spoken to and heard the experience of such who lived then, can realise how great a terror there was in the land. Terror there might be, and was; but not paralysis. Though hearts might quake and faces blanch, yet heads planned and hands executed all that was thought prudent or necessary for defence. To this threat, and a feeble echo of it some thirty years ago, we owe our Volunteer Army. The people were anxious to qualify themselves to resist the enemy, and volunteer corps were formed in nearly every town and village. In order to provide uniforms, &c., and prevent too great a strain on the Imperial Exchequer, Independent Volunteers paid for their own equipment, while Corporate bodies and wealthy individuals subscribed largely to a National Fund. The Hull Corporation on the 12th of January, 1798, under Jno. Sykes, Esq., Mayor, subscribed £500 for the service of the

the State, and the Wardens and Brethren of the Trinity House subscribed a like sum."*

Regarding the Hull and Cottingham Volunteers, the *Hull Advertiser* of July 5th, 1794, says, "We are happy to hear that the equipment of the Independent Volunteers of this town [Hull] is in a state of great forwardness. The uniform will consist of a blue jacket faced with scarlet, white waistcoat, nankeen trowsers, black gaiters, and a round hat with feathers: the buttons are to have the impression of the Hull Arms upon them." There were also paid volunteers, and the Trinity House established an Artillery Volunteer Corps.

Volunteer Corps were formed at Patrington, Hornsea, and Leeds. At the latter place, "On Wednesday last, [January 6th, 1796] the Leeds Gentlemen Volunteers were reviewed by H.R.H. Prince William of Gloucester, on Chapel Town Moor"; † and in the paper for the 16th of the same month we find that the Prince resigned the command of the troops in the Yorkshire Division of the North-East District to Lieutenant-General Scott. Wednesday, February 17th, 1796, was the day fixed by General Scott for the consecration of the colours to be presented to the Hull and Cottingham Volunteers by Sir Samuel Standidge, Knight, ‡ Mayor of Hull and Warden of the Trinity House; but beyond saying that they were a very handsome pair of colours, they were not described in the newspaper.

Beverley also formed a splendid corps, which was larger, better equipped, and sooner ready to take the field than the corps of Hull and Cottingham.§ Their colours were presented by the Corporation, and one of them bears the

* "Hull Advertiser." Jan., 1798. † Ibid., Jan. 9, 1796.

‡ Son of Robert Standidge, Bridlington Quay. He died Feb. 10th, 1801, aged 76 years, and was buried in St. Mary's Church, Lowgate, Hull. For portrait and further particulars see Wildridge's "Old and New Hull" (pp. 37, 40).

§ "Hull Advertiser," Jan. 16, 1796.

Beverley Arms and the motto "*Pro Rege et Patria.*" These colours are now placed in the Percy Chapel, in Beverley Minster, over the tomb of the fourth Earl of Northumberland, and near the helmet of Harry Hotspur. *

The above-mentioned Lieutenant-General Scott made energetic efforts to render his district safe, as proved by the following Regulations for Owthorne District, which are here printed *in extenso* :

"COPY OF REGULATIONS FOR NO. 4, OWTHORNE DISTRICT.

"MR. BURRELL, WITHERINGSEA.†

"Head Quarters, Beverley, April 9th, 1797.

"The Preparations making upon the Coasts of Flanders and Holland, with the avowed Resolution of Carrying Devastation and Rapine into such Parts of Great Britain or Ireland, as may best suit the unprincipled ambition of the Present Rulers of France, makes it indispensibly necessary (from the uncertainty of the Point to which the Efforts of France will be directed) that the Coast of Holderness, which lies so immediately exposed to the Enemy, should be Put into such a state of Preparation for defence, as under the Divine Protection may render ineffectual, and finally defeat every attempt on the Part of our Inveterate Enemies, and that with united Hands and Hearts we may defend and secure our Invaluable Liberties and Property against all Invaders.

"In order to Prevent as far as may be, the confusion and distress that may arise in case of an actual Invasion taking Place, Lieutenant-General Scott has, in the first instance, established a chain of Posts and Patroles on the Coast from Bridlington to the Spurn, in order that an early intelligence of the appearance of any enemy may be immediately circulated throughout the whole district, and that every Person interested, and who is to stand forth in defence of his

* "Eastern Morning News," July, 1886. † Withernsea.

country may, without delay, repair to his Proper Post of Alarm. That the different Points may be Perfectly known, the General has divided the Coast of Holderness into 13 small districts, each of which is Put under the more immediate Care of a Principal Person residing in it, who is denominated Captain of a District, and to whom the Regulations and Directions necessary to be followed and observed are given, in order that they may be circulated and made known by each Captain to the Principal Persons and all others, who are resident in the several Towns and Villages in each District, and it is hoped that the best effects will follow from every Person being occupied in forwarding the business of his own Particular District, and in executing the orders and directions that will be fully, and it is hoped, clearly explained, upon every article relating to the different Districts, and agreeable to their respective situations, and it is earnestly desired that the Captains of Districts and the Principal Inhabitants in each, will frequently peruse the Proposed Regulations, and that they will impress upon the minds of their Neighbours, Servants, and Labourers the necessity there is, and the advantages that must follow from the expeditious and Punctual Observance of what will be required from them.

"The Following Instructions are Principally To be attended to in the several Districts.

"DRIVING THE COUNTRY.

"It being of the utmost importance that all horses, Cattle, and every other thing necessary for the service and subsistence of an enemy should be removed from the Coast, as expeditiously as Possible when the appearance of an enemy in Force upon any Part of the Coast shall be clearly discovered, and which must, from a variety of Signals, and other circumstances that will appear, be clearly ascertained by the Captain and Principal Persons in each District, the whole of the District will Turn out accordingly. The

Horses with their Harness must be collected without loss of Time in such place as may be fixed upon by the Captain of the district in order to be disposed of in such manner as the different services may require.

"It will be most advisable that Cattle of every Description should also be collected with all Possible Expedition. That they should be classed seperately and drove off either in Flocks or Herds as by that arrangement each seperate division and species of Stock will be removed with the most expedition and Regularity.

"GRAIN AND FLOUR, BACON, ETC.

The Grain that is actually thrashed out and the Flour that may be in the different Mills should be secured and carried off with as much expedition as Possible. For this Purpose a sufficient number of Waggons or Carts should be fixed upon, who are to repair to such Barns or Mills on the first Alarm, that they may be loaded accordingly and drove off in Time to escape being seized for the use of the Enemy, as also all Bacon, &c., that may be in store. These articles may be conveyed to such Places where any body of troops may be assembled, and would be disposed of for the subsistence that would be wanted for the different Corps, and for the reimbursing the Proprietors, so that as little loss may be sustained from their removal as may be.

"STACKS OF GRAIN.

"The removal of Stacks of Wheat, Barley, or Oats, &c., would be attended with so great a loss of time, and the many impediments their removal must unavoidably occasion on the different Roads, makes it absolutely necessary that they should be burnt the moment the advance of the enemy may endanger their falling into their hands. The Carrying this measure into execution will be left to the discretion of the Captain of each District, who will receive the necessary orders from the Lieutenant-General. Government having engaged to make good all losses on this head, it will be necessary, that accurate returns of the Stock of Grain actually in being, should from Time to Time, be given to the Captain of each District, who will transmit them to the Lieutenant-General, at Beverley, in order that the Real loss and value may be ascertained, and the quantity actually destroyed may be known, which value it is Proposed shall be regulated by the Prices of Grain at the Last Market Day, Prior to the Time Such Stacks may be destroyed.

"No Persons however will be indemnified for any loss that may be occasioned by the Fireing of their Stacks, who do not also direct the driving of their Cattle, and who do not Join their Neighbours and Friends for the defence of their Country and Property, and contribute their best endeavours to harass the enemy by every means in their Power, and which may be Pointed out to them by such Officers, as will be appointed to direct them as circumstances may require.

"SERVANTS AND LABOURERS.

"A list of the number of Servants and Labourers in each district should be made out as soon as conveniently may be, and kept by the Captain of each District, who is desired to make such a disposition of them, as their numbers will admit of, and as they may be most Properly Qualified for, viz :—

"1st. The Number wanted to attend the waggons and carts, that may be employed in removing Grain, Flour, &c.

"2nd. The Number wanted for driving and attending the Horses.

"3rd. The Number for driving oxen, Cowes &c of that Species.

"4th. The Number for driving Sheep of all descriptions.

"5th. The Number for driving Swine of all descriptions.

When these services are Provided for, if any remain, they should be furnished with necessary impliments for the

Breaking up Roads and Bridges, Felling Trees, or if capable of using any Fire Arms, in all which cases, they will be Put under the Immediate Directions of such Officers as may be best spared from the Regulars, and who will be able to direct them, so as to retard the Progress and otherwise harrass the Enemy in every direction, as he may advance into the Country, from their knowledge of the different Roads, that will enable them perhaps to surprize and disconcert the motions of the enemy with comparatively a small degree of Hazard and danger to themselves.

"POINTS TO WHICH HORSES, CATTLE, AND STOCK ARE TO BE DIRECTED.

"The Particular Points to which every thing is to be driven will be specified in the directions that will be given to the Captains of the several Districts, but as the object the Enemy will most Probably have in view will be the destruction of the Dock, and Shipping, and the Pillage of the Town of Hull, every exertion must be made for the Protection of that Important Place.

"It will be absolutely necessary that the army assembled for this Purpose should be Properly and regularly supplied with Bread, Meat, and Forage; consequently the first directions will be that sufficient supplies for this Purpose, shall in the first Instance be directed to take their Position behind the River Hull, and the Town of Beverley. Future movements must depend upon circumstances as they may arise, upon the Force the Enemy may bring forward, and the success that may attend their operations.

"It will however be of the utmost importance that the Captains of the Districts immediately on the Sea Coast, should attend to the motions of the enemy, and whether they may Point more immediately towards the shores near Easington and the Spurn, in which case the utmost Expedition must be used in clearing that District, other Districts will have more Time, the same will be the case if Sandly Mer* should be their first object, so that by this Cool and determined Line of Conduct, should the attempt be made at Hornsea, every object will be answered and the whole business of the Country may be effectually executed without hurry and confusion, which must unavoidably happen, was it to be Put in motion at the same Time indiscriminately, as the General Stock of the whole must be very considerable indeed, and was it to meet in certain Points, the whole might be endangered, whereas by strictly observing the Regulations now intended to be established, the several Districts may move in succession to different Points which the several Captains of Districts, assisted by the Principal Persons residing in them may regulate before the Hour of danger may arrive. It must always be remembered that the Principal Roads leading from Hull to the Coast are to be left as clear as possible for the Passage of the Troops and Artillery, and it is hoped that Care will be Particularly Taken that all Stock, &c., shall be driven by such roads as may be equally convenient, and which must be well known to the occupiers of Ground in the Different Districts.

"As soon as these Regulations are circulated thro' the several Districts of Holderness, the Lieut. General means to arrange other districts in order that Proper and sufficient Preparations may be made for the reception of what may be collected from the different districts on the Coast, &c.

"*(Signed)* GEO. SCOTT, Lt.-Genl."

People still living can point out the situation of the camps for the patrol, placed in some hollow, so that the tents could not be seen from the sea; and it was reckoned no ungodly thing to do, to muster after service in the church, to take musket and bayonet and prepare one's self to fight for the

* About two miles north of Withernsea, now a dry sandy hollow, from which the sea is excluded by a bank.

dear old country; while the figure of a Frenchman was chalked on a barn wall, or his effigy erected in the middle of a ten acre field, on which was perfected the aim of the enthusiastic volunteer.

Careful housewives had all their valuables packed in bundles to be ready for instant removal, and, said an old lady, "After taking off my spectacles, and tying them and my Bible in the special bundle, which lay near my bed head, I used to look across the country to Bainton Beacon to see if it was alight; for we were always fearful that we should be aroused at night, because of the landing of the French, and hurried away to a more secure place."

Children, during the day, were forbidden to play far away from home, for fear they should be absent when most required; and the most wilful and turbulent of them was awed into a terrified obedience by being told that the Frenchman would get him.

For weeks and months in the Middle-street, at Driffield, there stood a row of waggons from the Buck Hotel to the Stocks in the Market-place, the site of which is now occupied by the large gas-lamp lighting the Market-place. These waggons were all numbered, and were intended to convey the women and children westward across the River Hull, or even across the Derwent. Mr. Chessman, of Patrington, remembers that his father's waggons were appointed for a similar purpose, though other waggons were required as per Instructions above.

There were many false alarms, which kept people nervous and unsettled, and sent affrighted women and children, half dressed and hysterical, to these sheltering waggons; but no false alarm in this district was so complete as that recorded in Chambers' "Book of Days,"* when, on the evening of the 31st January, 1804, a beacon on Hume Castle, in Berwickshire, was lighted in consequence of a mistake, and, other

* Vol. I., p. 200.

beacons following the example, the volunteers throughout nearly all the southern counties of Scotland were in arms before next morning, and pouring fast to their respective places of rendezvous.

Some particulars of this affair have been set down by Sir Walter Scott, who had opportunities of observing what happened on that occasion. "The men of Liddesdale," says he, "the most remote point to the westward which the alarm reached, were so much afraid of being late in the field that they put in requisition all the horses they could find, and when they had thus made a forced march out of their own country, they turned their borrowed steeds loose to find their way back through the hills, and they all got back safe to their own stables." These Liddesdale men entered Kelso with their pipes playing the lively tune:

"O wha dare meddle wi' me!
An' wha dare meddle wi' me!
My name it is little Jock Elliot,
An' wha dare meddle wi' me!"

Another remarkable circumstance was the general cry of the inhabitants of the smaller towns for arms, that they might go along with their companions.

The Selkirkshire yeomanry made a remarkable march, for although some of the individuals lived 20 or 30 miles distant from the place where they mustered, they were, nevertheless, embodied and in order in so short a period that they were at Dalkeith, which was their alarm post, about one o'clock on the day succeeding the first signal, with men and horses in good order, though the roads were in a bad state, and many of the troopers must have ridden 40 or 50 miles without drawing bridle.

The invasion seemed imminent when Napoleon, who had now assumed the title of Emperor, appeared in the camp at Boulogne. "Let us be masters of the Channel for six hours," he is reported to have said, "and we are masters of the world." A skilfully prepared plan at once to divide the English fleet and combine the whole French navy was frustrated, for

> "The best laid schemes o' mice and men
> Gang aft a-gley,"

and Nelson's decisive victory at Trafalgar, on the 21st of October, 1805, dissipated all danger. "England expects every man to do his duty" ran Nelson's famous signal, and though he himself fell in the hour of victory, twenty French sail had struck their flag ere the day was done.

In order to supply the army lots were drawn by the men, to determine who had to serve in the army, and he upon whom the lot fell had to leave all and prepare himself for warlike service, unless he could find a substitute or pay a fine. Men formed themselves into Ballot Clubs ("Ballad Clubs" they were called), and subscribed weekly, to form a fund out of which was paid a substitute to take the place of one or more of the members who "fell." Mr. Thos. Boynton, of Thornham, says that for four or five years he paid £2 or £3 yearly in subscriptions to his "Ballad Club."

The country was so drained of able-bodied men that only boys and aged men were left to do the necessary field-work. An old man said to me, "Ay; awd men were vallyubble then."

The Press-Gang was the chief agency to supply the navy, and greatly was it feared, for men never felt safe from its power unless they had a Protection Order, which was, in many cases, only for a limited period, say three or six months.

But even with a Protection Order there was not always safety, for if the gang urgently desired to have a suitable person, they did not scruple to steal his Order, and then seize him because he had no Protection.

The following is a permanent Protection Order, and is

now in the possession of Mr. Jas. Spencer, 18, Walmsley Street, Hull :

No. 40.  J. Ferraby, Printer, Butchery, Hull.

These are to Certify whom it may concern, That the Bearer hereof,

James Spencer, aged 19 years, middle stature, fair complexion, wears his own light hair loose,

Is one of the Seventy Men employed by Messrs. Westerdell and Barnes, Shipwrights, at Hull, and entered in their Protection.

Dated the Sixth day of October, 1787.

(Signed) T. WESTERDELL & BARNES.

CHAPTER III.

BEACON SITES AND RELICS.

THE various beacon sites and relics of East Yorkshire here follow, in alphabetical order.

ALDBORO'.

Aldboro', or Aldborough, had three beacons in 1588, and the beacon in the 18th and 19th centuries stood on Bunker's Hill. It is marked on Bryant's map of East Yorkshire (1829), and was the same shape as Mappleton, and somewhat like Hunsley Beacon.* It was removed about 1825 or 1830.

ATWICK.

In Elizabethan times there was no beacon at Atwick, but in more modern times one was erected on Collier Moor Hill. It was like Patrington Beacon,† having pegs through the post for steps, and a grate at the top of the post for holding the keg of tar. On Teesdale's map of Yorkshire (1834) it is marked T shape, like Holme Beacon; and on Bryant's map of East Yorkshire (1829) it is shaped like Dimlington Beacon; but my authority for saying it was like

* See engraving of Hunsley Beacon. † See illustration of Patrington Beacon.

Patrington Beacon is Mr. Jno. Coates, of Atwick, who remembers it well, and who has climbed up it many a time.

On sheet 180 of the 6in. Yorkshire Ordnance Survey it is called Moor Hill Beacon; while in Phillips' "Geology of Yorkshire"* it is called Skirlington Beacon.

This beacon stood about 60ft. above high water, and remained until 1855 or 1860, when it fell from decay, or was removed when the field was placed under cultivation.

AUBURN.

"Washed away by the sea" is the epitaph of many a village along the Holderness coast, and Auburn is one of them. The only relics are a farm house and a solitary cottage, very near the edge of the cliff; but this village, with the adjoining hamlet of Fraisthorpe, had, in 1588, "three beacons, a myll from the sea, taking lighte from Bridlington, and giving lighte to Houlderness."

Because of its poetic beauty and local reference, I have been constrained to embody in this work the following poem on "Auburn," by the Rev. Richard Wilton, M.A.†

Here Auburn stood
By pleasant fields surrounded,
Where now for centuries the ocean flood
With melancholy murmur has resounded.

Here Auburn stood
Where now the seabird hovers—
Here stretched the shady lane and sheltering wood,
The twilight haunt of long-forgotten lovers.

The village spire
Here raised its silent finger,
Sweet bells were heard and voice of rustic choir
Where now the pensive chimes of ocean linger.

* Vol. I. p. 66.

† "Modern Yorkshire Poets," by Wm. Andrews, F.R.H.S., p. 5.

Dear white-faced homes
Stood around in happy cluster,
Warm and secure, where the rude breaker foams,
And winter winds with angry billows bluster.

Here, in still graves,
Reposed the dead of ages,
When lo! with rush of desecrating waves,
Through the green churchyard the loud tempest rages.

Here Auburn stood
Till washed away by ocean,
Whose waters smile to-day in careless mood
O'er its whelmed site, and dance with merry motion.

Here now we stand
'Mid life's dear comforts dwelling;
Soon we shall pass—Oh, for a Saviour's hand
When round our "earthly house" Death's waves are swelling.*

BAINTON.

In 1588 Bainton had "two beacons, takinge lighte from Ruston, and geveth lighte to Hunsley and Wilton." As there are two Bainton Beacon sites (one old, one new), we can fairly suppose that the beacon on the old site was the 16th century one. On the left hand, or south side, of the road from Kirkburn to Bainton there are Beacon Wood and Beacon Farm; but the growth of this wood prevented the light of the beacon from being seen at Driffield, so the beacon was removed to a field across the road, to the north side, and placed 20ft. higher, making it nearly 180ft. above the sea-level.

Mr. Simpson Staveley, of Eastlands, Tibthorpe, sends me word that he was told by an old villager that this beacon consisted of a single post, with a cage at the top to hold the tar-barrel.† From Mr. Henry Angas, of Driffield, who was

* Revised by the Author. † See Patrington Beacon.

born on "Beacon Farm," I gather that there was a heap of stones round the base of the beacon, and that some of these stones were built into the end of a barn, while one huge one is used as a mounting-block at the entrance to the farm-yard.

As no one seems to remember, or be able to say, whether it had the usual pegs for steps, it seems probable that the watchman, standing on the cairn, was able to reach the barrel without going higher.

The field is arable, and has been cultivated for many years; so that this would necessitate the removal of the cairn, the post, and the barrel, and now the name and memory alone remain. Bainton Beacon was seen by Mr. Francis Pearson, of Driffield, in 1828; but it is not marked on either Bryant's or Teesdale's maps, constructed from actual survey in 1829 and 1834 respectively.

The Rector of Bainton (Rev. J. W. Stanbridge, M.A.) has generously sent me the following interesting extract from the Bainton parish registers: "Elizabeth, daughter of Thomas Blackburne, the soldier at Bainton Beacon, and Elizabeth his Wife, was baptized, October 4th, 1807."

This beacon, like those of Holme, Wilton, and Hunsley, gives its name to a Division of the Riding.

BARMSTON.

Barmston was a beacon-station in 1588, and had three beacons, which gave light to Bainton and Rudston.

The modern beacon stood on Hamilton Hill, which, though not very high, is a prominent object for miles around, and stands near the coast, about three-quarters of a mile north of Barmston.

This beacon, which was destroyed some 40 or 50 years ago, consisted of a pole with blocks of wood nailed on the sides, at short intervals,* to enable a man to climb up conveniently, and an arrangement of hoops, etc., at the top for holding a

* See engraving of Rudston Beacon.

tar-barrel. There was also a hut adjacent to the pole for the men in charge, whose names were Skinner and Hill, both Skipsea men. The Barmston men had rejected with scorn the offer of one guinea per week, which was the usual payment for that service: but they were very envious when they saw these two men, shoemakers by trade, earning their regular wages at their own work, and receiving, in addition, such a large sum for watching the beacon. There is a stone let into the ground to indicate the spot where the beacon used to stand. Mr. Holliday, an aged farmer, at Barmston, says that his father remembered all the beacons about here being lighted occasionally for trial or practice.

The Barmston sands were so well known (through extensive smuggling operations) and were so well adapted for landing boats, that the people in the village seem to have quite made up their minds that the French would land there. Once, indeed, active preparations were made for quitting the place, and some families actually started.

BOREAS HILL.

At Boreas Hill, near Paull, there is a Beacon Field, which is so called from its having been a beacon site. This Beacon Field is mentioned in the Instructions of 1588.* This beacon stood in the S.E. corner of the field, and was similar to Patrington Beacon, having in addition four stays. There is nothing of it now, but it was one of the last in this district.

BRIDLINGTON.

"Bridlington-cum-Key," saith the old document, "hath three beacons uppon the sea cost, geving lighte to Flambroughe and Fraistroppe."

In this neighbourhood the sea has made great inroads upon the land, and many and many a broad acre has been

* See p. 9.

washed away by the rolling billows when urged by a fierce north-easter. Visitors to Bridlington may see to-day evidences of this encroachment in the broken sea-wall. The grass field next to this, now cut up into building lots, is called the Beaconsfield Estate, and Mr. Jno. Browne, of Bridlington, says it is so called because the beacon stood therein. This name is the only memorial of the beacon, and I have been unable to find anyone who ever saw it.

COWLAM.

In Elizabethan times, Cowlam, or Coleham, had one beacon "taking lighte from Staxton and Bridlington, and geveth lighte to Settrington. Some affirm that yt may be sene as farre as Hornsey in Houlderness."

Of this one, or any other beacon at Cowlam, there is now no trace whatever, either in name, "stick, stone, or staver." The Rev. Geo. N. Herbert, Rector of Cowlam, surmises that Kemp Howe would be the place selected, because, though not the highest point, it is so favourably situated that from its summit a vast district can be seen, with the light of the Flambrough lighthouse, the chimneys of Hull, and the highlands at Settrington on the line of the horizon. This tumulus—Kemp Howe—was opened by Mr. Mortimer, of Driffield, some years ago, but no trace of any beacon relic or foundation was then to be seen. If ever it had been there, all had been entirely removed; but the present very good state of preservation of this Howe leads one to suppose that it, and it alone, must have been preserved for some purpose, and that purpose we believe was a beacon site.

DIMLINGTON.

Dimlington, in 1588, had "three beacons, all uppon the sea cost, and do geve lighte to these beacons following uppon Humber."

The land on which these and the later beacons stood is

now all washed away. The beacon, at the beginning of this century, and even so late as 1840 or '50, stood on the top of Dimlington Highland, for it is marked on sheet 257 of the 6in. Yorkshire Ordnance Survey, on Bryant's map of East Yorkshire (1829), and also on Teesdale's map of Yorkshire (1834). On all of these it is the same shape as the illustration.

Dimlington Highland was chosen as a suitable place for the formation of a camp, and here some hundreds of soldiers were held in readiness to resist the landing of the dreaded Frenchman. Mr. Martin Kemp, an ancestor of the present Kemps, in Hull, supplied the camp with beef, &c.

There was also a camp at Tunstall, in 1794-5, which was garrisoned by the Durham Militia, with a park of artillery.*

DRINGHOE.

Thos. Boynton, Esq., Ulrome Grange, says "Last year [1885], Canon Greenwell and myself explored a hill, at Dringhoe, which we expected was a barrow, but we found no traces of burial. There were, however, two large oak trees crossing each other at right angles, and forming a framework, either for the foundation of a mill or beacon, probably the latter."

FLAMBROUGH.

"Flambrough, three beacons uppon the sea cost, takinge lighte from Bridlington, and geving lighte to Rudstone." So saith the old instructions of the days of good Queen Bess.

In Napoleonic times fewer would suffice. The venerable pile of weather-beaten, storm-eaten chalk stones, called the "Old Lighthouse," gleaming ruddily in the rays of the setting sun, or looming dim and spectre-like through the ocean mists blown landward, if able to speak, could doubtless tell us of anxious hearts keeping a vigilant outlook from

* Poulson's "Holderness," Vol. II. p. 88.

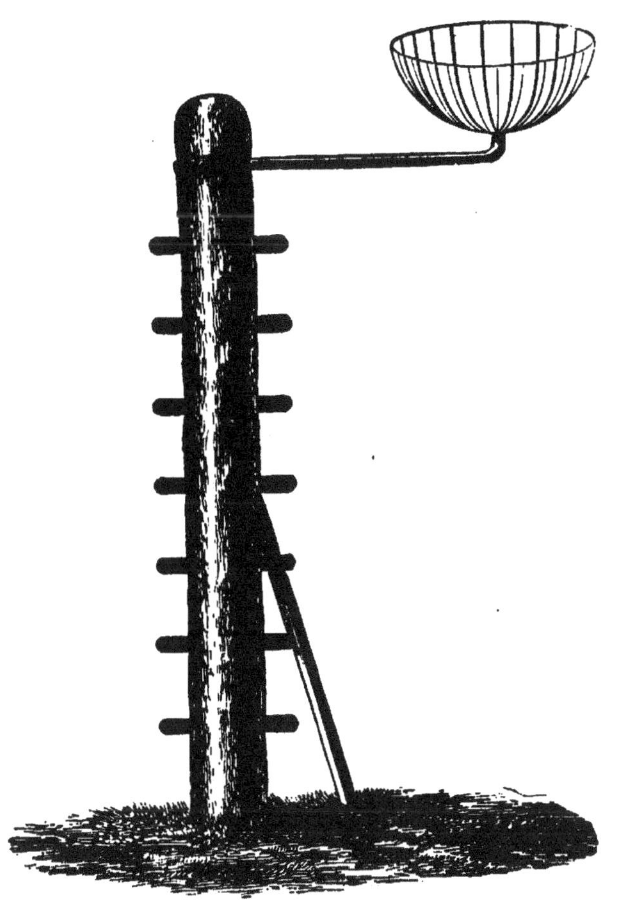

DIMLINGTON BEACON.

(ABOUT 1830).

Now Washed Away.

its summit; not only for the hostile fleet of France, three generations ago, but for that of Spain, three centuries ago. It has always been the "*Old* Lighthouse;" and people look upon it as one of the things that always was, like the mighty headland with the stones of which it is piled. On the top of it is a fireplace or recess for a cresset used for burning a light.

Overlooking Bridlington Bay, and near the south end of the Danes' Dyke, is a large circular mound, which bears the name of Beacon Hill. On the highest point of this hill the site of the beacon is still more or less distinctly to be traced by means of the stones yet remaining of the cairn which stood around its base, or of which the watchmen's hut was built. It was there in 1834, was T shaped, like the one at Holme-on-Spalding-Moor, and is marked on Teesdale's map of Yorkshire (1834), but of the wood or ironwork there is no trace now. The farm on which it was still bears the name of Beacon Farm.

In Plillips' "Geology of Yorkshire,"* on the coast section, there is a beacon marked at the north end of the Danes' Dykes. It is called the "Old Beacon," but there is nothing left of it now. The place is most suitable, but no name of any kind is there, as a memento, though a local tradition assigns a beacon to the huge mound that forms the rampart at the north end of the vast earthworks popularly ascribed to the fierce Northmen.

FRAISTHORPE.

At Fraisthorpe there is a Beacon Hill, and nothing more, to recall to mind the beacon which once stood there.

GRIMSTON.

The beacon of Grimston, in Holderness, stood near Garton, on a hill still called Beacon Hill; but there is now no trace

* Vol. I., p. 32.

of it. About 60 years ago it was in existence, and consisted of a pole with the barrel of tar on the top, as at Hunsley and Aldborough.

There was also a beacon at Hilston. I am told that the tower on Hilston Mount was used for that purpose, but on Teesdale's map (1834) the beacon is marked close to the sea, and of the same shape as the Dimlington Beacon. Hilston Mount was used as a hospital for the troops during their encampment on this coast, in 1794-5.

HOLME.

Holme beacon, in Elizabethan times, "taketh lighte from Hunsley and Wilton, and geveth lighte to Marchland and the Lowe Cuntreyes." The only traces of this beacon are the slight mounds in the pasture-field, about one hundred yards south of the church, which mounds cover the foundations of the short brick pillars that served as bases for the supports of the upright beam. Dr. R. Wood, of Driffield, supplied me with the sketch from which the illustration was engraved, and its accuracy has been verified by old inhabitants of the place. An old man (whose name has not been given me), 84 years of age, who was for many years Clerk of the Church, remembers that his uncle was one of the night watchmen in charge of the beacon, and he still sees it, in his mind's eye, as he saw it long years ago, charged with tar-barrels ready for use, and we to-day may be thankful that its dread message was not flashed over our beloved country, probably soon to be followed by the greater blaze and denser smoke of burning homesteads and flaming stack-yards.

At one time it was painted white, as though some person were anxious to preserve it; but it gradually decayed, and was finally blown down in a gale of wind about 1840-5. During the last few years of its existence it formed a splendid plaything for the boys of the township, who loved

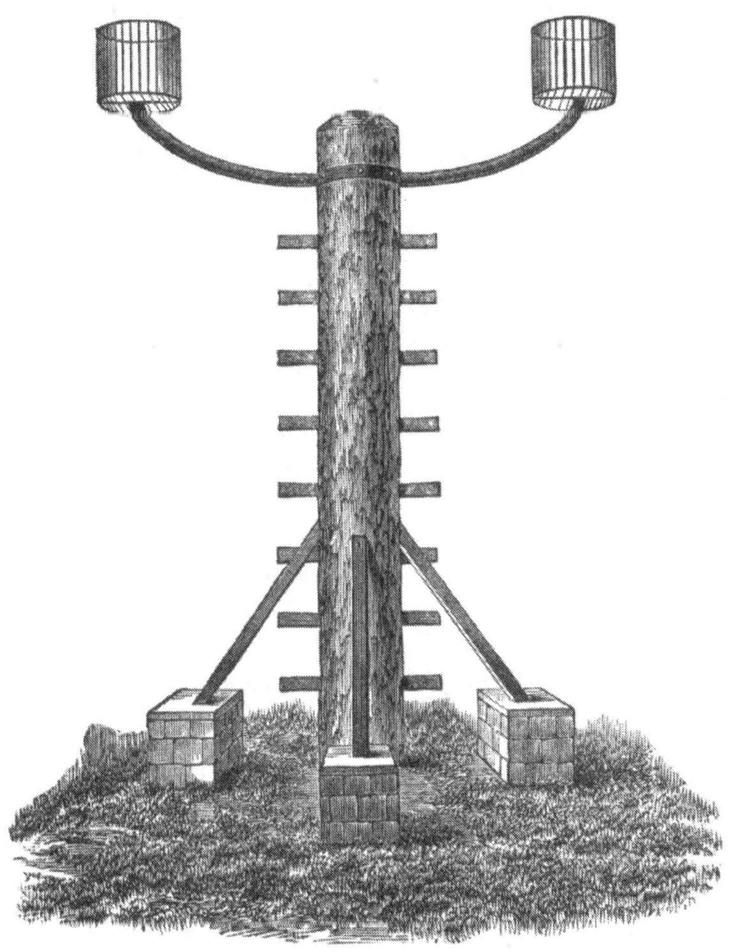

HOLME BEACON.

(About 1840-5).

From a sketch supplied by Dr. Richard Wood, Driffield.

to race up its spiny sides, and shout their glee from the two grates on its arms. Ah! children often find sport where their fathers found anxiety.

This beacon is marked the correct shape on Teesdale's map, already referred to, dated 1834-5.

The church at Holme, standing on a boss of sandstone, is a well-defined object in the landscape for miles around, and is known among the hunting brotherhood by the name of "the visible Church of Christ on earth."

One of the cressets of this beacon shewed marks of having been used, thus confirming the statement* that they were all lighted occasionally for trial or practice.

HORNSEA.

Hornsea had, in the 16th century, "three beacons, further upon the sea cost in Houlderness," which "geve lighte to Bainton and Rudstone."

The site of Hornsea Beacon is now washed away. On sheet 197 of the 6in. Yorkshire Ordnance Survey the site is marked a few hundred yards north of the Marine Hotel, Hornsea, and a short distance from the cliff, so as to be covered with the sea at high-water. The Beacon is not marked either on Bryant's map (1829) or on Teesdale's map (1834).

In 1794-5, there was a camp on the west side of Leys Hill, so far down that the tops of the tents could not be seen from the sea. Hornsea was then unenclosed. The garrison at first was a regiment of Northumbrians, and afterwards a regiment of West Yorks.

HUNSLEY.

When it was feared the Spaniards would invade this country, Hunsley had "two beacons, takinge lighte from Bainton, and geveth lighte to Holme;" but during the 300

* See Barmston Beacon.

years when we had no fear of foreign invasion they would in all probability disappear.

From about 1798 to 1820 or 1830, this beacon stood at the highest point of the road from Drewton to High Hunsley, in the corner of an arable field. In this case, a shallow tub took the place of the usual cage, at the top of the pole, which was supported by three tall props reaching nearly to the top. The steps to reach the barrel were cross pieces of wood on one of the supports.

The engraving was taken from a sketch made from a description given by Mr. J. Boodie, of Hull; but there are several old people living at South Cave who remember having seen it, both erect and during the time it lay on the ground, previous to its final removal and destruction.

KILNSEA.

Kilnsea was a beacon station three centuries ago, and to-day there is only a Beacon Hill, marking the site of the signal post. This hill is marked on Bryant's map of East Yorkshire (1829), while the beacon itself is marked on Teesdale's map of Yorkshire (1834), and on sheet 269 of the 6in. Yorkshire Ordnance Survey (1840). On both it is of similar form to Dimlington Beacon*

This beacon stood about 140 feet above high-water mark, on the top of a cliff composed of clay, with pebbles scattered through it. †

MAPPLETON.

The beacons at Mappleton and Aldborough were simply upright poles, with the tar-barrel on the top, and were in existence until about 1826; and so were the little huts of sods, erected for the shelter of the beacon-watchers. The kindly Vicar of Mappleton (Rev. T. W. Kelly), sends me

* See illustration of Dimlington Beacon. † Phillips' "Geology of Yorkshire," Vol. I. p. 61.

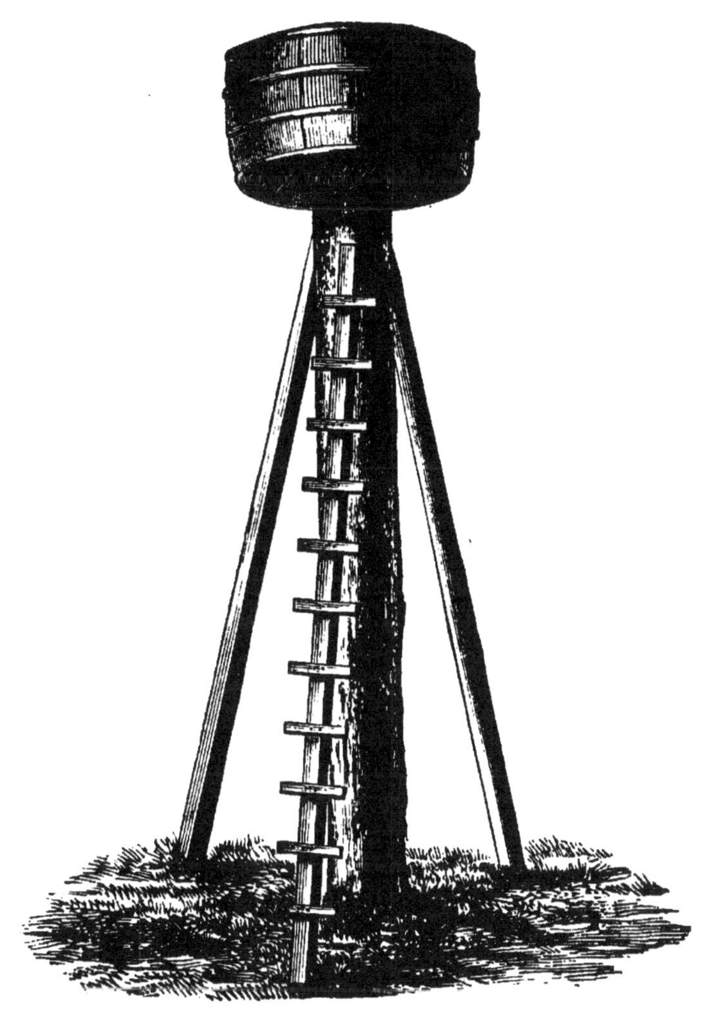

HUNSLEY BEACON.

(About 1830).

From a description by Mr. J. Boodie, Hull.

word that an old man informed him that these huts were very comfortable, and were occupied by a sentinel even in his day, long after the people had settled down to their ordinary work and ways.

MUSTON.

"Muston three beacons, half-a-myll from the sea cost, taking lighte from Righton, and geveth lighte to Staxton."

The more modern beacon was removed about 1809. It also was T shaped, like Holme Beacon, and stood on a hill a little to the north of Muston, still called Beacon Hill.

The beacon is marked on Teesdale's map of Yorkshire to which reference has been made so often; and the site is marked on sheet 110 of the 6in. Ordnance Survey of Yorkshire. On Bryant's map of East Yorkshire (1829) it is marked of the same shape as Dimlington Beacon.

NUNBURNHOLME.

The gardener of the Rev. J. W. Stanbridge, Vicar of Bainton, recollects, though imperfectly, a beacon which stood on the top of Nunburnholme Wold. The woodwork appears to have been a triangular pyramid, the cross pieces from one pole to the other being a few inches apart, and forming three ladders, one on each side, reaching to the top, on which was a receptacle for the barrel of tar. I have not yet been able to confirm this statement. The present navigation beacon at Kilnsea is somewhat similar to the above description.

OWTHORNE OR WITHERNSEA.

Owthorne beacon stood in a grass-field about half-way between North Cliff Farm and Sandley Mere. It had two arms like Holme Beacon, but the site and all have long ago been washed away. The steady encroachment of the sea is at the rate of about six feet each year.

PATRINGTON.

Patrington beacon, with those at Welwick, Bowerhouse-Hill, Paull, and Marfleet, were "the beacons standinge uppon Humber, and takinge lighte from the beacons aforesaid [those upon the sea coast from Grimston to Kilnsea] do geve lighte to the beacons in Hartil and Hulshier, which are Transbye and Hunslay."

To-day the only memento of Patrington Beacon is the name Beacon Hill, given to a slight elevation on the road, about half-way to the Haven. The beacon stood in a small square field, two or three hundred yards from the Haven Mill and about half-a-mile S.W. of the church. This beacon was *repaired* in 1803. There was no new one erected; so it is a fair conjecture to say that one must have stood there since the 16th century. There are several aged inhabitants now living at Patrington who well remember seeing it, and the mud hut, close by, for the beacon-watchers. It was standing until about 1820, when it was pulled down; and the boards affixed to it, containing the directions for firing the beacon, were used in building hen-roosts at the East-End Farm. The beacon consisted of an upright post, about 10ft. high, with projecting "pinns," or pegs, for steps on either side, and on the top of the post was the cage for the barrel, ready to be lighted at any moment the signal might be made.

Whilst speaking of Patrington Beacon, I desire to express my gratitude to the Vicar of Patrington (Rev. H. E. Maddock) for his untiring exertions in procuring information for me, which is both valuable and interesting. It was he, also, who obtained from Mr Kirkwood the Proclamation made in 1797. The clergy generally in the East Riding have, in this matter, proved efficient, willing, and generous helpers, and my best thanks to them I tender.

At Welwick, on a piece of ground called "Ploughland," there stood a beacon of the same shape as the one at

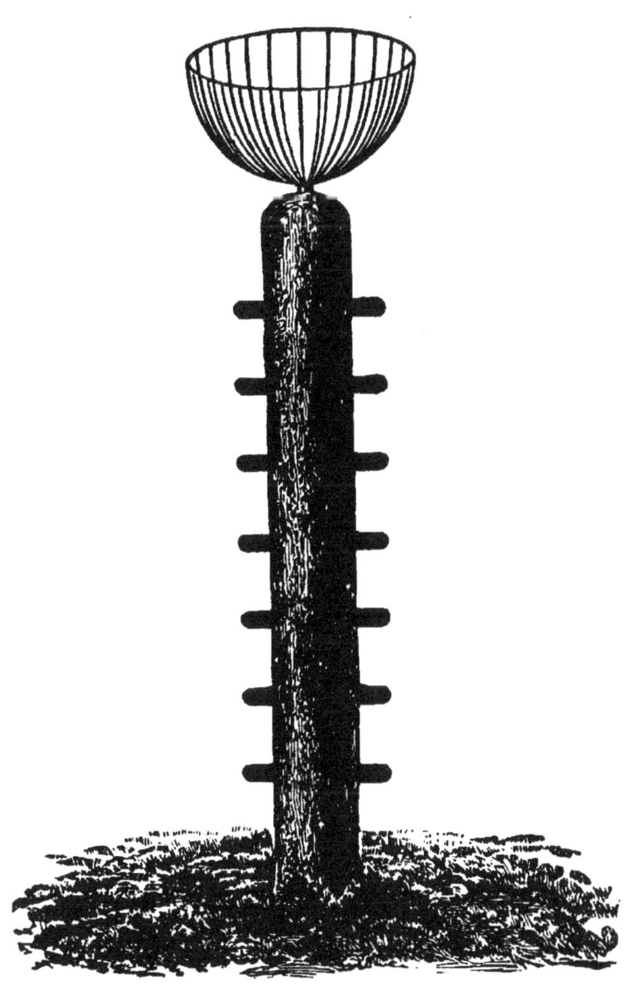

PATRINGTON BEACON.

(About 1820).

From a description by Mr. Parrot and Mr. Chessman, of Patrington.

Patrington; and in 1820 there was one on the road side, half-way between Ottringham and Winestead, of the same shape, but both these have disappeared.

The sketch of the Patrington Beacon was made from descriptions given by Mr. Robt. Parrot, of Patrington Haven, and by Mr. Harrison and Mr. Chessman, of Patrington.

PAULL.

This was a beacon-station in Armada times, and afterwards, in 1809, the beacon stood on the cliff top, not far from the Humber. It consisted of a short thick mast, with crosstrees, on which stood two tar-barrels, one on each side, close to the mast. Affixed to the mast, was a top-mast, which displayed a flag, probably shewing the same signals as at Spurn.* From this it appears that the flag would be used during the day, and at night the barrels would be ignited. But their ignition would be the destruction of the beacon, for there was no provision to guard against it. However, should a second fire be needed, a large stack of wood was piled close at hand, and ready for immediate use.

The cliff on which this beacon stood is now washed away; but Mr. Jas. Spencer, Hull, well remembers both the cliff and beacon.

RUDSTON.

The modern Rudston Beacon stood on the top of a tumulus, a little to the north of Wold Gate, a few hundred yards before turning to the left to descend the hill to the pretty little village of Rudston, with its interesting church and monolith enthroned on the summit of a hill.

On sheet 145 of the Yorkshire Ordnance Survey the tumulus on which the beacon stood is marked "Rudston Beacon," and near it is Beacon Plantation.

* See Spurn Beacon.

Mr. Robt. Boynton, of Thornholme, and Mr. and Mrs. Thos. Edmonds, of Burton Agnes, remember the beacon standing. It consisted of a tall thick tree, with "chocks" of wood nailed on the sides, forming steps, to enable a man to reach the tar-barrel, which hung in a flat-bottomed cage, suspended from an iron bar by a strong chain. The hut for the beacon-watchers was made of sods, and stood at a short distance from the beacon.

A man, named Tom Taylor, of Rudston, had charge of the beacon for some years. He was paid a guinea a week for his services, and, said Mr. Robt. Boynton to me, "We used to be mad to think that he could earn as much as we could at turnip hoeing, and have his guinea a week besides."

The beacon seems to have been removed about 1825 or 1830, but the hut of sods remained a few years longer; and, if I remember rightly, there is still a slight mound to mark its site.

The Rev. Canon Taylor, M.A., of Settrington, sent me a sketch of this beacon as it was in 1809, which had been copied from an old map of Burton Agnes. It stood just outside the parish of Burton Agnes (Wold Gate being the division between the parishes of Burton Agnes and Rudston), but the land on which it stood is owned (and, I believe, farmed) by a Burton Agnes farmer.

In this sketch, the hut was shewn as being close to the beacon, and the cage for the tar-barrel could be raised or lowered by means of a cord and yard-arm, thus dispensing with steps or ladders. None of the old people who had seen Rudston Beacon would admit of this arrangement, but as there is an interval of about ten years between their recollection of it and the date of the sketch, it might have been altered in the meantime.

RUSTON.

Ruston Beacon, three hundred years ago, was "six mylls

RUDSTON BEACON.

(About 1825).

From descriptions by Mr. Robt. Boynton, of Thornholme, and by Mr. and Mrs. Thos. Edmonds, of Burton Agnes.

from the sea cost," took "lighte from Rudstone," and "giveth lighte to Bainton Beacon."

The modern beacon, apparently, stood on the site of the old one, on the high ground in the angle of the road from Driffield to Kilham. It was a prominent object, and would be well known to the coachmen and guards of the "Wellington," "Express," "Magna Charta," "British Queen," and other coaches, for it stood on the side of the road from Driffield to Bridlington. Mr. John Browne, of Bridlington, remembers it; and says "It would be the last of the beacons that remained in this district, and was removed between fifty and sixty years ago. My recollection of it is that it was a tall pole, with a tar barrel at the top, and had projecting steppings to reach the barrel, something like this."

Mr Browne's sketch is very much like the illustration of Patrington Beacon.*

On Bryant's map of East Yorkshire (1829), this beacon is marked as being similar to Dimlington Beacon.†

SETTRINGTON.

Settrington beacon "taketh lighte at Coleham and Scarbrough and geveth lighte to Whitwell beacon, and all that way to Yorke, and into Harthill, and over the most part of Pickering Lythe."

There is now nothing left of this beacon, save the name given to a tumulus, 651 feet above the sea-level, on the High Street leading from Thirkleby to Settrington. The Rev. Canon Taylor, M.A., says that on a rough calculation it commands a view of over 400 square miles, including the Grand Stand on Scarborough race-course, round by the North and West to York Minster and the hills beyond Selby.

It is marked, as being in existence, on Sheet 125 of the Yorkshire Ordnance Survey, and also on Bryant's map (1829), and from eye-witnesses I gather that it was shaped

* Page 47. † Page 35.

like the beacon at Dimlington.* It was removed about 1830-40.

SKIPSEA.

Skipsea, being near the sea, like other coast towns and villages, had, in the days of Elizabeth, "three beacons uppon the sea cost in Houlderness, to geve lighte to Bainton and Rudstone."

All that ever was of the Skipsea Beacons has long since been washed away. There is no site or commemorative name either on Bryant's map (1829), Teesdale's map (1834), or the Ordnance Survey Sheets. There was no beacon known as Atwick Beacon in the 16th century, and that beacon may have been one of the Skipsea Beacons, although Atwick is not in Skipsea parish.

STAXTON.

Staxton Beacon took light from Muston and gave light to Cowlam. A Beacon Hill, near Ganton, marks the site of this Beacon. Seamer Beacon is not far away, and the iron beacon on Scarborough Castle wall is still in existence.

SPEETON.

"Righton-cum-Spetonn, three beacons on the sea cost, takinge lighte from Flambroughe, and geveth lighte to Rudstone." So in century sixteen.

'Twas a pleasant bright day when two of us left Driffield, by rail, to visit Speeton, to see the relic of the old beacon. Arriving at the lonely station, our inquiries for direction elicited, in addition to what we wanted, looks which, interpreted, might be read "Are these fools or madmen! to travel thus far to see a bare, weather-beaten stump, on the top of a high hill!" Yes, the hill was steep, and the time was brief, but when the summit was reached and we stood, with one arm

* See illustration of Dimlington Beacon, page 35.

SPEETON BEACON.

(In 1886).

From a sketch made on the spot by the Author.
When complete it had two arms, like Holme Beacon.

round the post, our feet on the cairn of stones at its base, and feasted our eyes on the pictures before us, we were well repaid. Almost at our feet rolled the mighty ocean, every billow foam-crested ; to the left, Filey Brigg, the legendary work of Thôrr or the Devil, pierced the bosom of the deep like a needle, and the angry billows fretted and chafed and foamed in vain around it; then Filey, and its amphitheatre of lovely arable and woodland country, with the horizon bounded by wolds and moors; now the little village Board School, half way between Reighton and Speeton, and as the children wended their way homewards, their laughter and cheerful voices reached us even up there.

Examining the beacon relic, we find it to consist of an oak beam, about 9 feet high, with six holes through it, in which had been fixed the pegs to form the steps. Round the bottom of the post is a great heap of large stones, and on the side away from the sea is a sort of rectangular space on which the grass grows poor and thin. This is probably the place where stood the hut which sheltered the watchmen.

When complete, the beacon had two arms, like those at Holme-on-Spalding-Moor, Flambrough, and other places ; though on Bryant's map (1829) it is shewn like Dimlington Beacon*

There is a legend that at one time the site of the old beacon was much nearer the village, and that the beacon was removed to its present position, farther away, because the inhabitants feared that, if lighted, it might be a danger to their stacks and homesteads.

On the hillside is a plantation, bearing the name of Beacon Plantation.

This hill, 450 feet high, is known as Raven Hill, and not far away, at Bempton, is Standard Hill.

Speeton Beacon, and probably all the others from Scarborough to Flambrough Head, were lighted when the

* See illustration of Dimlington Beacon, p. 35.

redoubtable Captain Paul Jones appeared off this coast in 1779, with four vessels, carrying 124 guns, and manned by nearly 1,100 men. His primary object was the capture of the fleet of Baltic merchantmen, but the Yorkshire people were greatly afraid of his landing, and militia were drafted into the coast towns to resist him. Thanks, however, to British pluck, he neither effected a landing nor captured one merchantman. Captain Richard Pearson, in the *Serapis*, 44 guns, and Captain Percy in the *Countess of Scarborough*, 20 guns, had charge of the Baltic fleet, and with true courage, they, at once, put themselves between their convoy and their enemy, in spite of superior numbers and weight. It was about 7.20 on the evening of the 23rd of September, 1779, "that the largest ship brought to, on our larboard bow, within musket shot. I hailed him and asked what ship it was. They answered in English, the *Princess Royal.* I then asked them where they belonged to. They answered evasively, on which I told them that if they did not answer directly I would fire into them. They then answered with a shot, which was instantly returned by a broadside, and after exchanging two or three broadsides, he backed his top-sails, and dropped upon our quarter within pistol shot, then filled again, put his helm a-weather, and ran us on board upon our weather quarter, and attempted to board us, but being repulsed, sheered off."* The two vessels afterwards became entangled, and for two hours they fought "so close fore and aft, that the muzzles of our guns touched each other's sides."† During this deadly struggle the *Serapis* took fire ten or twelve times, and as many times was with difficulty extinguished. Making matters worse, about half-past nine, an explosion "blew up all the people and officers that were quartered abaft the mainmast, and rendered all these

* Captain Pearson's Despatch, written on board the *Pallas*, French frigate, in Congress service, Texel, October 6th, 1779.

† Ibid.

guns useless for the remainder of the action, while one of the frigates kept sailing round us the whole action, and raking us fore and aft, by which means she killed or wounded almost every man on the quarter and main decks."* For more than an hour after the *Countess of Scarborough* had been captured by the *Pallas*, 32 guns, Captain Pearson fought on single handed, until the fall of his mainmast by the board, with nearly all his crew *hors de combat*, and seeing it "impracticable to stand out any longer with the least prospect of success,"† he struck. Captain Pearson and the first lieutenant were then escorted into the enemy's vessel, which they found to be the *Bon Homme Richard*, 40 guns, and 375 men, out of which number 306 were either killed or wounded. "Her quarters and counter on the lower deck were entirely stove in; the whole of her lower deck guns were dismounted; she was also on fire in two places, and six or seven feet of water in her hold, which kept increasing all night and next day, till they were obliged to quit her, and she sank with a great number of her wounded people on board her."‡ After paying a high compliment to his officers and men, and to Captain Percy, who "was not the least remiss in his duty,"§ Captain Pearson concludes "I am extremely sorry for the misfortune that has happened, that of losing his Majesty's ship I had the honour to command; but, at the same time, I flatter myself with the hope that their lordships will be convinced that she was not given away, but, on the contrary, that every exertion has been used to defend her, and that two essential pieces of service to our country have arisen from it—the one in wholly oversetting the cruize and intentions of this flying squadron; the other in rescuing the whole of a valuable convoy from falling into the hands of the enemy, which must have been the case had I acted otherwise than I did."‖

* Captain Pearson's Despatch. written on board the *Pallas*, French frigate, in Congress service, Texel, October 6th, 1779.

† Ibid. ‡ Ibid. § Ibid. ‖ Ibid.

Captain Pearson was afterwards knighted for his bravery, and both he and his gallant colleague, Captain Percy, had the freedom of the borough of Scarborough presented to them in two boxes made of heart of oak, elegantly decorated with silver, and bearing suitable inscriptions.

The night of the action was bright and moonlight, and the battle was witnessed by hundreds of people on the top of Flambrough's lofty cliffs, which were often struck by shots from the conflicting vessels.

SPURN.

The Beacon at Spurn is thus described in the *Hull Advertiser* of 24th June, 1796. "The Trinity House issued the following:—On Monday last, the 21st of June, a flag staff was fixed on the lower light at the Spurn Point, from whence the following signals are ordered to be made on the appearance of an enemy.

"1st.—A blue flag, when an enemy is upon the coast, and her exact situation not known.

"2nd.—A blue flag with a red flag above it, when to the South.

"3rd.—A blue flag with a red flag below it, when to the East.

"4th.—A union flag with a red flag below it, when to the North."

WILTON.

Bishop Wilton beacon "taketh lighte from Bainton, Hunsley, and Ruston, and giveth lighte to Holme beacon, to the cytty of York, and to the lowe cuntreye."

On Sheet 159 of the Yorkshire Ordnance Survey (dated 1854) and on Bryant's and Teesdale's maps (1829 and 1834) this beacon is marked as being in existence, but when Mr. Mortimer, of Driffield, opened the tumulus, in June, 1866, there were left only the foundations of the beacon, transverse beams, of great thickness, laid in position a few feet below the surface.

The beacon stood on the top of Garraby Hill, 780 feet above the sea-level, and consisted of one upright post, having pegs projecting from the sides to serve as steps, and on the top was the iron cage to receive the requisite tar-barrel.*

During the fear of the French invasion, two watchers, named Gray and Black, lived in the hut made of sods, which stood near the base of the beacon. In 1823, a farmer, entering on a farm near the beacon, took away some of the iron, to work up in making a waggon. The work of spoliation once begun, others assisted until it finally disappeared, but not until 1850 or 1855.

Near this tumulus are Beacon Field and Beacon Road, the latter of which is about 800 feet above the sea-level, and commands an extensive view.

WRESSLE.

Wressle Castle was rendered "inteneable"† by order of the Council of State, in 1650. Three sides of the castle were demolished, but the whole south front remains "flanked by two square towers, and these again are mounted by circular turrets of a smaller size. Upon the top of one of the turrets is still preserved the iron pan of the beacon."‡ The iron framework, which served to hold the beacon-pan, was there in 1805.§ At the present time there is no iron pan or framework, nor has there been such for many years, but the stone coping shews where the iron was affixed.

This completes the list of the Beacons of the East Riding of Yorkshire.

* See Patrington Beacon, p. 47.

† "History of Wressle," p. 48. ‡ Ibid. p. 50. § Ibid. p. 50.

During the last two or three years, the enquiry "Have you seen a beacon?" has been constantly on my lips. Though varied have been the answers, none so completely non-plussed me as the one from a rustic, "Naw! Ah nivver seed yan! What's it like? Is it sum sooat ov a hanimal?"

Even those who live in the constant presence of a name-relic know very little of the beacon. You may enquire of dozens of people living near some Beacon Hill, or Beacon Farm, and they can tell you nothing, save that the name was always so, they suppose; and you will finally be directed to some "old inhabitant" that "knaws summat aboot it." The old man proves to be one who perhaps was once a sailor but who is now well nigh blind, and of little service as a member of society, though, as you question him, you find his mind clear; and a long-forgotten light sparkles in his eyes, and a brighter red enlivens the ruddiness of his weather-beaten cheeks, under the excitement of the memory of the "brave days of old," when his father took him to the watcher's hut, for company, when he used to stand by the beacon post, and climb up its sides, to watch for the appearance of the enemy on the sea, where they were too afraid to go and fish, for fear of being surprised and captured. But his failing strength brings back the remembrance of his long life,—he shakes his head despondingly; sighs deeply; and lapses into a silence which you feel ought not to be broken; while you depart, glad that it has been your privilege to live for a few minutes in the history of the past.

The days of beacons are over. A few more years and there will be no one living who ever saw one; and personal recollections will be impossible to get. Their memory is fast departing; and their name, which will soon be their only relic, will carry with it little significance, because of the departure of the reality; but should a like danger threaten us, we might do worse than repair or re-erect the beacons which, for rapidity of transmission and dissemination of their message, are scarcely surpassed by more modern discoveries and inventions. The electric telegraph may excel in transmission, but the beacon light must bear the palm for dissemination.

Our forefathers were very thankful that the French fleet did not put in an appearance, for soon it would have been seen that

A sheet of flame, from the turret high
Waved like a blood-flag from the sky
        All flaring and uneven;
And soon a score of fires I ween,
From height, and hill, and cliff, were seen;
Each with warlike tidings fraught;
Each from each the signal caught;
Each after each they glanced to sight,
As stars arise upon the night,
They gleamed on many a dusky tarn,
Haunted by the lonely earn;
On many a cairn's grey pyramid.
Where urns of mighty chiefs lie hid.

APPENDIX A.

In "Britannia Depicta," fourth edition, 1736, which shows all "ye Direct and Principal Cross Roads, in England and Wales," there are marked the following beacons :—

Page 16. Dreaton Beacon (Notts).
" 20. Gateshead Beacon.
" 42. Beacon near Tilbury Marsh.
" 42. Beacon on Shooter's Hill.
" 42. Beacon on Gillingham Hill near Rochester.
" 43. Ospring Beacon near Rochester.
" 43. Bocton Beacon, 6 miles from Canterbury.
" 46. Beacon on Stanway Marsh, near Colchester.
" 46. Harwich Beacon, also on p. 199.
" 70. Alderton Beacon.
" 70. Newhaven Beacon.
" 70. Another Beacon, 6 miles from Newhaven.
" 96. Longdon Beacon, 6 miles from Midhurst, Surrey ; also on p. 252.
" 96. Singleton Beacon, 4 miles from Chichester.
" 104. A Beacon 10 miles north of Lincoln.
" 104. Barton Beacon (Linc) on the top of Beacon Hill. It seems to be something like a tripod,* having steps fastened on each pole, and from the top there is an arm supporting a sort of cage or cresset.

* See Hunsley Beacon, p. 43.

Page 104. Elsom Beacon, a few miles from Barton, and having a beacon of similar shape to Barton Beacon.

„ 105. About 5 miles from Bridlington, and near Burton (Agnes), there is a beacon marked, consisting of an upright pole with cross pieces for steps, and having a cage, with a round bottom, at the top of the pole.* Though the situation is not correct, this is probably Ruston Beacon.†

„ 113. Baldock Beacon.

„ 117. Hockum Beacon, 18 miles from Norwich.

„ 159. Beacon near Brington, Northamptonshire.

„ 167. Brecknock Beacon—apparently a square tub on the top of a pole.

„ 177. Tiverton Beacon.

„ 177. A Beacon 19 miles from Exeter.

„ 178. Ilfracombe Beacon.

„ 195. Codnam Beacon, 7 miles from Ipswich, also on p. 199.

„ 195. Yaxley Beacon 21 miles from Ipswich.

These two last are both alike, and similar to Barton Beacon, above.

„ 199. Shotley Beacon.

„ 207. Nottingham Beacon.

„ 216. A Beacon near the vale of the White Horse.

„ 229. Ressington Beacon, near Stow.

„ 252. Deal Beacon.

„ 252. Langdon Beacon.

„ 269. Runswick Beacon, near Whitby.

„ 272. Whitwell Beacon, 14 miles from York. This beacon is referred to in the Certificate of Beacons in the East Riding, 1588.‡

* See Patrington Beacon, p. 46. † See p. 50. ‡ See p. 9.

HALIFAX GIBBET AND BEACON.
(Supplied by Wm. Andrews, Esq., F.R.H.S.)

APPENDIX B.

The block from which the above engraving has been printed was kindly lent by Wm. Andrews, Esq., F.R.H.S. Though the chief object in it is Halifax Gibbet, it is of interest and not wholly out place in this work because it shows the position and shape of Halifax Beacon, on Beacon Hill. The Beacon is almost a facsimile of Patrington Beacon* and helps to confirm the shape of the receptacle of the tar-barrel, to which exception has been taken, as being unsuitable and unsafe.† This shape is further confirmed by the sketch of a beacon on p. 105 of "Britannia Depicta."‡

* See p. 46. † See p. 14. ‡ See p. 66.

INDEX.

THOS. HOLDERNESS, PRINTER, DRIFFIELD.

www.ingramcontent.com/pod-product-compliance
Lightning Source LLC
LaVergne TN
LVHW020035170826
845678LV00001B/273

* 9 7 8 0 3 5 3 3 4 1 2 6 5 *